"Turtle"

by Nick Baker

2018
NB
and
Kathy Parag

To Kathy Passage, my mom and Number One Fan...I am YOUR Number One Fan!

Kim Kimmy: Without you there would be no book called "*Turtle*". Thank you for being interested in my life, telling my story, and getting my words onto pages so that they can be shared with everyone.

Deona Koberstein: My best ever job support coach, who demonstrated over and over again an ability to think outside the box! Your ability to make sense of the story and get the illustrations in order helped so much to get us to the finish line and into print.

Elizabeth Malek, a.k.a. Aunt Lizzie: Thank you so much for reading and rereading and taking yet another look at my story and helping Mom look at the pictures, since I could not see them.

Susan and Jeff Jones: Your love and support has spanned the years. I've grown from being your student to you two becoming my lifelong friends.

Ray Passage: Mom and I both thank you for your patience and support.
I know there were times when dinner was a bit late or you brought home take-out from the deli so Mom could keep working on the book.
Thanks, Man!

Requests for permission to make copies of any part of the work should be submitted online at info@mascotbooks.com or mailed to Mascot Books, 560 Herndon Parkway #120, Herndon, VA 20170.

PRT0515A

Printed in the United States
Library of Congress Control Number: 2015939383
ISBN-13: 978-1-63177-267-2

www.mascotbooks.com

"Turtle"

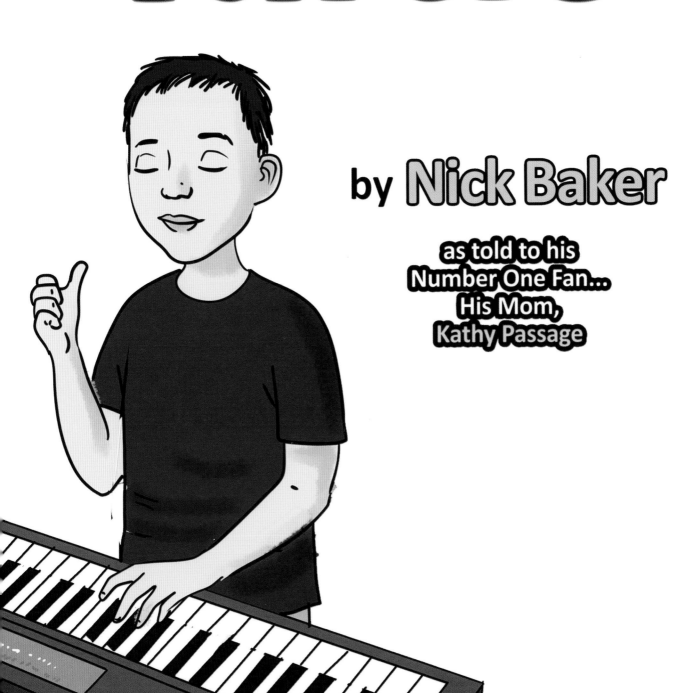

by Nick Baker

as told to his
Number One Fan...
His Mom,
Kathy Passage

My name is Nick Baker. I have Autism, and I am blind. Autism is a pretty big word. It means that my brain probably works a little differently than yours does. I want to tell you a story about something that happened to me when I was a little kid.

In some ways, I am just like you. I went to school just like you. I liked learning and wanted to make friends just like you. In that way, we are the same.

In other ways, we are different.

I walk with a cane because I am blind. My cane has a red tip. I tap the ground in front of me as I walk. My cane lets me know if a step or bump is coming, so I won't trip or fall. This is one of the tools I have to keep me safe.

Because of my Autism, I had a special assistant at school named Mrs. Weber. Mrs. Weber came to each class with me to take notes and help me understand the class assignments.

Using a cane and having a special assistant makes me different from you.

Having Autism also means that I might not understand your jokes. I don't always know what to say. Being blind means I can't see the expressions on your face. If I can't understand jokes and can't see people's faces, it can be hard for me to make friends.

Sometimes being different is fun. One way it's fun is when you have a talent. Having a talent means that you can do something special and that you do it well.

I have a special talent. It's music! I love to sing and play the piano. I also love to perform. My mom thinks I'm pretty good, especially because I have perfect pitch, which means my voice sounds the same as the keys played on the piano.

My mom is my Number One Fan! Do you know what being a fan means? I am a fan of Stevie Wonder and Pharrell Williams, which means I really, really love their songs. Whenever I hear their music, I feel super happy. Do you have a singer or TV performer that you like very much?

I may not understand a joke or be able to see, but I can play songs and remember all the words after hearing them just one time. I'm grown up now, but I could do this even when I was a little kid, before I started school.

I feel lucky to have this special talent!

For a long time, I didn't know that most people couldn't do this. Can you do it? Try it!

Now that I am a grownup, I perform all the time, but even when I was a little boy, I enjoyed singing and playing piano in front of people. It is kind of hard to have your hands doing something like playing the piano while you are trying to remember the words to a song. Can you pat your tummy and rub your head at the same time? It is sort of like that.

Even though I have this special talent, sometimes kids in school didn't understand me. They thought I was weird and that made me sad. Kids called me names and teased me because I was different. That hurt my feelings. I felt lonely.

Do grownups sometimes say to you "Stand up and walk straight"? I walk funny. I can't see, so I have to use my ears to listen extra hard to everything around me as I walk with my cane. I turn my head from side to side and stick my neck out in front of me as I go along. Kids at school said I looked just like a turtle sticking its neck out of its shell. They would shout "Turtle! Turtle!" when they saw me walk by.

Another reason kids at school made fun of me is because loud noises really scare me. Sirens and alarms make my heart race and my body shake. Mrs. Weber used to take me outside before fire drills started and the loud alarms started ringing. When she took me outside, kids would shout "Turtle is a Scaredy Cat!" Kids thought it was unfair that I got to go outside first. I thought it was unfair that I was so afraid of loud noises. I couldn't help it – it's just how I am.

Sometimes I wished the kids would stop teasing me. I wished they would appreciate my special talent instead of making fun of me for being different. I really wanted kids at school to like me. I wanted to be their friend. What could I do?

Our school principal, Dr. George, loved to have her students share their special talents with the rest of the kids in school and with the parents, too. Sometimes we would have programs on stage in the auditorium and our parents would come to watch us perform. Every year, Dr. George made a video recording of all the programs showing us kids singing and playing.

Did you know that blind people "watch" TV? I can't see the pictures, but when I watch, I am actually listening to the sound. My mom saved the videos of all the school programs. I love to listen to them. I laugh like crazy when I hear my high-pitched, squeaky voice from when I was eight years old.

Have you ever noticed that grownups have lower voices than kids?

In one of my favorite videos, I played a reindeer in a holiday program. I had lots of fun shaking the jingle bells and singing "Rudolph the Red Nosed Reindeer".

You probably know that Rudolph was teased too. He was different because he had a red nose.

One day at school, I learned that we were going to have another
talent show! It was a contest that anyone could enter and there was a
prize for the best act!

I wanted to play the piano and sing all by myself like I had done
last year. I thought maybe if I sang and played the piano well, other kids
would like me.

Then something happened to change my plan.

As I was walking to lunch, I heard some girls singing with a boom box. The song was "Hit the Road, Jack" by a famous guy named Ray Charles. Ray Charles was a blind singer who played the piano. *Hey, he's kind of like me*, I thought, *except I have Autism*.

Sometimes I forget my manners. Do you ever do that? I do this more than you probably do because of my Autism. I interrupted and started singing the parts that Ray Charles would sing. I forgot to ask permission before I did that!

Has a grownup ever asked you not to interrupt?

When I started singing, it was quiet for a minute. I was worried. The girls laughed and shrieked at me, "Turtle! Who asked YOU to sing?"

That really hurt my feelings!

Mrs. Weber said something that made me feel better. She asked the girls, "Do you plan to sing this song at the talent show?"

"Oh, yes. We want to play the recording of Ray Charles singing and we will sing the girls' part," they said.

Mrs. Weber had a great idea. "Would you like to have Nick sing with you at the talent show? He could even play the piano or an electric keyboard."

There was another long pause...

Then the girls finally said, "Well, maybe that would be okay. It is kind of cool that Nick already knows the words to the song. Maybe he could play it on the piano, too!"

Whew! When the girls said that, it made me feel a whole lot better.

Plus, I already knew how to play that song on the piano.

Mrs. Weber thought it was a good plan. "Let's get together in the music room tomorrow and hear how you all sound," she suggested.

I was excited...until we started to practice!

It was very hard for me to sing with the girls. I had trouble being patient while they learned the words, as I already knew them.

I shouted, "OH, NO!" when the girls started to sing their part at the wrong time.

One girl started to cry.

I felt sad because I had hurt their feelings. I know that everybody makes mistakes. I wanted these girls to be my friends. I did not mean to hurt their feelings, but my Autism outbursts sometimes make me sound mean. Plus, I really wanted to win that contest!

I was glad Mrs. Weber was there to help. "Be patient, Nick," she reminded me.

We worked really hard for two weeks. We practiced and practiced almost every day after school. The girls learned all the words and when to sing their parts.

Mrs. Weber helped all of us to be more patient and polite with each other. Because of that, I was making friends!

The big night came. My new friends and I waited backstage for our turn to perform. There were lots of people who were going to be watching us. I was excited because my parents and my big brother were in the audience.

Finally, it was time to take our turn in the contest. We each took a deep breath. We did our best.

Our hard work paid off, and we sang really well!

The girls did great and I felt so proud of my new friends! I knew I had done my best. I thought we sounded just like Ray Charles did on their boom box. I hoped it was good enough to win.

Suddenly I heard a loud noise, but this time I was not scared.
Do you know why? It was lots of clapping! Guess what happened!
My friends and I won first prize!

Some kids still called me "Turtle" and made fun of my walk, but these girls were my new friends and did not call me that again. When they saw me at school, they'd laugh and start to sing, "Hit the Road... NICK!"

Even today, some people still make fun of me and hurt my feelings. Can you guess what I do when that happens? I hum that song to myself. It reminds me that I have friends and that I am a winner!

Nicholas Alexander Baker 01/09/1981

Nick would like to share his stories with others. Being born totally blind and later in early adulthood being diagnosed with Autism, he experienced many challenges in his childhood and school years. Nick started writing original music in 2000. Many of his original songs have a story behind them.

In 2008, Nick graduated with honors from Shoreline Community College with an AA degree in Music Performance. Nick works in his home studio to write, record, engineer, and produce much of his music.

Although totally blind, he uses technologies that allow him to work independently. He earns much of his living by performing at assisted living facilities, local restaurants, wineries, and club venues.

Another one of his passions is creating jingles for radio and advertising.

Nick lives with his mom and stepfather, Kathy and Raymond Passage, in Edmonds, Washington, where he participates in community service work at the local senior center. He also visits schools and shares his music with students.

To hear Nick's music, please visit his website www.nickbakermusic.com.

REFERENCES:

There are many organizations we've found to be good places to start seeking assistance and information for families of children with visual impairments, Autism, and other disabilities. Many can direct you to local groups in your area.

Our BEST advice for parents of a newly-diagnosed child with any type of disabilities: You are the best advocate for your child. Educate yourself on your state laws and school district policies.

Here is an example of a very comprehensive document from Rhode Island. Your state will have similar information.
www.health.ri.gov/publications/
guidebooks/2011ForFamiliesOfChildrenWithAutismSpectrumDisorders.pdf

Some great organizations that offer lots of information and support in Washington and nationally:

Autism Action
www.autismaction.org

Autism Speaks
www.autismspeaks.org

Federation for Children with Special Needs
www.fcsn.org